A Job for George and Milo

Claire O'Brien

Illustrated by
Sarah Lawrence

OXFORD

OXFORD
UNIVERSITY PRESS

Great Clarendon Street, Oxford, OX2 6DP,
United Kingdom

Oxford University Press is a department of the University of Oxford.
It furthers the University's objective of excellence in research, scholarship,
and education by publishing worldwide. Oxford is a registered trade mark of
Oxford University Press in the UK and in certain other countries

Text © Claire O'Brien 2017

Illustrations © Sarah Lawrence 2017

The moral rights of the author have been asserted

First published 2017

British Library Cataloguing in Publication Data
Data available

978-0-19-837751-1

7 9 10 8 6

Paper used in the production of this book is a natural, recyclable product
made from wood grown in sustainable forests. The manufacturing process
conforms to the environmental regulations of the country of origin.

Printed in China

Acknowledgements

Author photograph by Deborah Ripley

Contents

Chapter 1
Tricked Again

George and Milo looked in the window of Mr Potter's shop. The best comic in the world had arrived. It was called *MegaBuzz*. If you had *MegaBuzz*, you could find out about:

MegaBuzz

Superheroes

Computer Games

Dangerous Animals

Secret Codes

Scary Masks – How to Make Them

Goals – How to Score Them

"It looks brilliant!" said Milo. "I wish I could buy it every week, but it's too expensive for me."

"Me too," said George.

Milo had lots of brothers and sisters so he didn't get much pocket money.

George didn't have any brothers and sisters, or any parents. He lived with his three aunts – Aunt Mash, Aunt Whizz and Aunt Bimm. They didn't have much money but they had lots of love and kindness.

George scratched his head. "There *must* be a job we could do to earn some extra money," he said.

George had tried to do helpful jobs at home but he wasn't very good at them. He really wanted to find a job that he could do well.

Just then, Nathan came out of
the shop with a copy of *MegaBuzz*.
Nathan was in George and Milo's
class at school. Everyone was scared
of him because he was big and bossy.
He pushed into queues and cheated at
games. Once, he even stole George's
pencil and snapped it.

"I bet you really want this comic, don't you?" he said to George and Milo. "Well, don't worry, you can have mine when I've finished with it."

George was suspicious, but Milo smiled and said, "Thanks, that's very kind."

Nathan grinned. "I'll just cut out the best pictures," he said. "Then I'll eat my chips off it. You can get it out of my dustbin."

And he walked away laughing.

Milo went red and squeezed his fists tightly. "Nathan always tricks me and makes me feel stupid," he said.

George gave Milo a pat on the back. "We *will* buy that comic," he said. "I promise. I'll think of a plan."

Chapter 2
Disappointment

The next day, George woke up with a brilliant idea for a job he could do to earn the money to buy *MegaBuzz*. He ran downstairs and into the garden to find Aunt Bimm.

"If I dig over the compost heap," George asked, "could I have some extra pocket money?"

Aunt Bimm shook her head and said, "Have you forgotten what happened last time?"

George would never forget it. He had got wriggly worms in his vest and then the compost heap had collapsed on top of him. His aunts had to dig him out.

"That wasn't the right job for you," said Aunt Bimm. "Think of something else."

George was disappointed, but he had another idea. He found Aunt Whizz. She was unwinding old woolly jumpers so that she could knit them into new ones.

"If I help you to unwind these jumpers," George asked, "could I have some extra pocket money?"

Aunt Whizz frowned and said, "Don't you remember what happened last time?"

George remembered it very well. He had got tangled into a zillion knots. It took his aunts an hour to untie him.

"That wasn't the best job for you," said Aunt Whizz. "Think of something else."

Again, George felt disappointed,
but he had one more idea. This time he
would have to ask Aunt Mash. She did
not like being disturbed so George was a
bit scared. He peeked around the door of
her shed.

DO NOT DISTURB!

"Aunt Mash?" he whispered.

"GO AWAY, GEORGE!" Aunt Mash
shouted. "I'm TRYING to tidy my shed!"

George went away quickly.

"It's no use asking her," he thought.
"And now I've run out of ideas."

That afternoon, George and his aunts cycled to the library. George had his own bicycle with a useful trailer. This gave him a new idea.

"If I carry all the library books in my trailer," he asked, "could I have some extra pocket money?"

Aunt Bimm sighed. "We tried that, George. Have you forgotten?"

George hadn't forgotten. He had raced through the park and hit a big stone. The books had flown out of the trailer and landed in a puddle. The librarian was very cross.

"Perhaps I could sell some things instead," George thought as he pedalled. When they got to the library he made a list.

MY THINGS	COULD I SELL THIS?	WHY?
My cars	No	I love them all!
My books	No	They are not mine, they belong to the library.
My old shoes	No	They have holes in the bottom.
My poster of Mick the Kick	No	It is signed and might be worth millions one day.

There was nothing he could sell.

"I will just have to keep trying to find a job," he thought. "There must be *something* I can do."

Chapter 3
Tasty Treats

George looked through lots of library books to get ideas.

"Perhaps there's a job that Milo and I could do together," he thought. He made a list and wrote down the good and bad things about each idea.

	IDEA	WHY THIS IS A GOOD IDEA	WHY THIS IS A BAD IDEA
1	Become pirates and steal treasure.	It would be an exciting adventure.	1. I haven't got a ship. 2. Milo gets sea sick.
2	Discover a cure for nits and verrucas.	It would help a lot of people.	1. We haven't got a laboratory to do experiments. 2. We might invent something dangerous and deadly by mistake.
3	Go on a TV quiz show and win some money.	We might win.	1. We might lose. 2. Children probably aren't allowed.
4	Make something that people want.	It might work.	

"That's it!" thought George. "We have to make something that people want and then sell it to them."

George made another list.

Things To Make That People Will Buy

1. Cheese
2. Shoes
3. Fancy hats
4. Portraits
5. Racing cars
6. Computers
7. Furniture
8. Treehouses
9. Fireworks
10. Plant pots

"Bother!" he thought. "All these things need *loads* of equipment and years of training. We need something quick and easy."

George was almost ready to give up when he saw a sign by the library door.

Tabletop Tasty Treats Sale
Bring your delicious
home-made treats to sell —
jam, biscuits, fudge,
chocolates, scones and cakes.
At St. Crinkle's Primary School,
Sunday 29th June, 2.30pm.
To book your table,
contact Mrs Elizabeth Smudge,
School Secretary.

"That's it!" he thought. "We'll bake lots of delicious cakes!"

Chapter 4
Disaster

Milo came to George's house that night for a sleepover. George told Milo about his cake baking idea.

"That's brilliant!" Milo said, with a big smile.

George looked at his calendar.

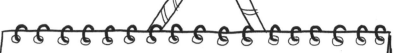

JUNE

MON	TUES	WED	THURS	FRI	SAT	SUN
	1 School holiday	2 Still school holiday	3 Still school holiday	4 Last day of school holiday	5	6
7 Back to school	8	9	10 Aunt Mash's birthday	11	12 MegaBuzz issue 1	13
14	17	18	19	20	21 MegaBuzz issue 2	22
23	24	25	26	27	28 MegaBuzz issue 3	29 Cake sale today 2.30pm
30						

"We have two whole weeks before the cake sale," he said. "That's plenty of time to become *excellent* bakers."

George and Milo explained the plan to Aunt Bimm and Aunt Whizz.

"It's a good idea," said Aunt Bimm. "But you mustn't touch the hot oven. I will put the cakes in and lift them out again."

"Yes," said Aunt Whizz. "We don't want any accidents."

George and Milo agreed.

"I'll call the school on Monday morning and book your tabletop shop," said Aunt Bimm.

But when George got home from school on Monday, Aunt Bimm had *disastrous* news.

"We have to *pay* to book a table before the sale," said Aunt Bimm. "But I don't have any money at the moment."

"Nor do I," said Aunt Whizz. "I'm so sorry."

George took a deep breath. "Don't worry. I'll ask Aunt Mash," he said.

"But she never gives money away," said Aunt Bimm.

"Not a penny," said Aunt Whizz.

"I know," said George, "but I've got a plan."

Chapter 5
A Careful Inspection

Aunt Mash was fixing a bicycle in her shed. George peeked in. It was still very messy. Everything was in the wrong place and Aunt Mash looked hot and bothered.

George whispered, "Hello."

"COME IN!" Aunt Mash shouted. "But DON'T get in the way. I'm VERY busy and I can't find a thing in this shed."

Aunt Mash had a list.

THINGS I MUST FIND
BIG SPANNER
MIDDLE-SIZED SCREWDRIVER
SMALL HAMMER
LONG SAW
BOX OF NAILS
GREEN SPRAY PAINT

George read the list and looked around. "I see the spanner!" he cried. "It's in the box marked 'paintbrushes'."

"Jolly good," said Aunt Mash. "But what about my middle-sized screwdriver? I bet you can't find that!"

George searched. He found lots of cobwebs. Then he searched behind a heavy tool bag. "Got it!" he called.

"Excellent!" said Aunt Mash. "I wish it were tidy in here. I get cross when I can't find my tools."

"If I tidy the whole shed for you," said George. "Would you pay me some money?"

"MONEY!" cried Aunt Mash. "What do you need MONEY for?"

George told her about *MegaBuzz*. He
told her about the plan to bake delicious
cakes for the Tabletop Tasty Treats Sale.
Then he told her that they needed to pay
for their table.

"Hummph!" said Aunt Mash. "I'm
not sure."

George was desperate. "I know my
jobs have gone wrong before," he said,
"but please give me a chance. I might be
good at tidying up *and* good at baking,
if you let me try."

Aunt Mash sighed. "OK, George," she said. "I'll give you a chance but I'll be back to CAREFULLY inspect your work in one hour." She looked strict. "And if you don't do a good job, I won't pay you anything. Do you understand?"

George nodded and got to work.
He put all the tools in the right boxes.
Then he put the tins of paint on the
shelves and sorted the nails, screws and
bolts into separate jam jars. Next, he
swept the floor and chased away three
enormous spiders. To finish off, he gave
everything a good dusting.

Just before dinner, Aunt Mash
returned. George was nervous. He held
his breath. What if she didn't think he'd
done a good job and wouldn't pay him?
What would he say to Milo?

But Aunt Mash was very pleased.
"That's not bad at all, George," she said.
"Well done."

George breathed out. "Phew!"

Aunt Mash gave him the money he
needed. George thanked her and rushed
off to find Aunt Bimm so that she could
book their table for the sale.

Chapter 6
One More Try

After school the next day, George and Milo started baking. Aunt Bimm helped them.

"Try this recipe," she said, opening her big book.

Aunt Bimm's Bouncy Sponge Cake

Ingredients

200 grams (1 cup) caster sugar

200 grams (1 cup) soft butter

4 eggs, beaten until fluffy

200 grams (1⅔ cups) self-raising flour

1 teaspoon of baking powder

2 tablespoons of milk

Method

Heat the oven to 190°C/375°F or 170°C/325°F for a fan oven or gas mark 5.

Beat the sugar and butter together until smooth and fluffy. *Never add chilli pepper.*

Add the eggs and beat for three more minutes.

Add the flour, baking powder and milk. Mix in gently. *No more beating.*

Pour the mixture into two cake tins. *Grease them first or the cake will stick.*

Bake for about 20 minutes. *Don't forget they are in the oven!*

Turn out and leave to cool. *Mind your fingers!*

Sandwich together with your favourite jam.

George and Milo worked very hard but their first cake was a *disaster*. It wasn't cooked in the middle.

"It's a squishy mess," said George.

"Perhaps baking isn't the right job for you after all," said Aunt Bimm.

"We can't give up," said Milo. "We just took it out of the oven too soon."

"May we have another try tomorrow?" George asked.

Aunt Bimm agreed and they tried again the next evening. But their second cake got burned. It was crumbly and black.

"I'm *really* not sure that this is the right job for you," said Aunt Bimm.

"*Please* can we have one more try?" George begged her.

"We mustn't give up on things just because they're difficult," Milo added. "We just left it in the oven too long this time."

Aunt Bimm sighed. "OK," she said. "You can have one final try tomorrow."

So the next day they read the recipe *extra* carefully and whisked the ingredients until they were *extra* fluffy. They baked the cake for exactly twenty minutes and Aunt Bimm turned it out gently. They had baked a perfect sponge cake. George and Milo cheered. Aunt Whizz and Aunt Mash rushed into the kitchen.

"What's happened?" asked
Aunt Whizz.

"Cake has happened!" said George.

They all tried a piece.

"Wonderful," said Aunt Bimm.

"Delicious," said Aunt Whizz.

"Not bad at all," said Aunt Mash.

"May I have some more?"

Chapter 7
Snatched!

It was soon Saturday again and George collected Milo in his bicycle trailer. Milo had a giant-sized packet of chocolate chips to add to their cake.

They stopped to look at the latest copy of *MegaBuzz*. The cover said:

MegaBuzz

See Super-Weird Fish from the Deepest Oceans

Measure a Tree Without Leaving the Ground

Make a Tyrannosaurus Mask

Build a REAL Bonfire

Free Computer Game – Aliens v Pirates. Which Are You?

"Oh no, here comes Nathan," said Milo.

"What've you got there?" Nathan demanded.

"Um ... er ... um ... chocolate chips," said Milo.

"I love chocolate chips," said Nathan with greedy, bulging eyes. "Give me those *now*."

"We need them for our cake," said George.

"I don't care!" said Nathan, and he grabbed the packet of chocolate chips and ran away. He was bigger and stronger than George and Milo so they couldn't stop him. Milo was so upset that his face went blotchy.

"Don't worry," said George. "We'll find other things to put in our cakes."

Back home, George looked in the
kitchen cupboard.

"I'll say an idea and you write it
down," he told Milo. Milo got his pencil
ready.

"How about sardine and raspberry
jam cake?" said George, and Milo made
a note. He wrote down George's other
ideas, too:

<u>Cake ideas</u>
Sardine and raspberry jam cake
Baked beans and chutney cake
Mint sauce and sultana cake
Cheese and onion crisps and pepper cake

"I'm not sure about these flavours," said Milo.

Aunt Bimm wasn't sure either. "I thought you were going to use chocolate chips," she said.

George told her that Nathan had snatched them.

"Did he indeed!" said Aunt Bimm. "What a greedy, bossy boy he is." She took her purse out of her pocket. "I have just enough money for you to buy some more," she said.

They hurried back to the shop but Nathan was waiting for them when they came out.

"Jump in the trailer, Milo!" shouted George. "Let's get out of here!"

But Nathan was on his super-fast racing bike. He smashed into the trailer and Milo fell out. The new packet of chocolate chips burst open. Chocolate chips flew up into the air and came down again like chocolate rain. Nathan rode away, laughing.

Aunt Bimm was very cross. "I shall
telephone your school first thing on
Monday about Nathan's behaviour," she
told them. "I will *not* stand for bullying."

Chapter 8
More Baking and
More Bother

Back at school on Monday, Nathan
was in trouble. He had to stay in at
playtime all week and learn extra
spellings, which he didn't like at all.
He had to learn:

technology technology television

actually digital

extinct believe

Martian curtain

accidentally explanation

Unfortunately, this didn't make Nathan behave any better. In fact, he got worse.

He chased George and Milo home from school every day, yelling, "I'm going to get you! I'm *really* going to get you two!"

On Thursday he chased them on his racing bike until George and Milo fell into a prickly hedge.

They both had scratches but it didn't stop them from baking. Every evening they made new flavours and tried new decorations.

On Friday, Nathan heard George and Milo talking about the cake sale. "You had better save your best cake for me," he said.

George was frightened but he didn't let it show. "You'll have to buy one, like everybody else," he told Nathan.

Milo's knees were knocking. "Yes," he agreed. "That's only fair."

"I don't care about what's fair!" Nathan shouted. "Save me the best cake or you'll be sorry next time I see you." And he stomped away.

"Phew!" said George. "We stood up to him this time."

"Yes," said Milo. "But what will he do to us if he doesn't get a cake?"

"Don't worry," said George. "I'll think of a plan."

Chapter 9
6 × 2 = Delicious

On the day before the cake sale George
and Milo baked twelve big, round
cakes. It was hard work but Aunt Bimm
helped them. There were two cakes in
each flavour. Aunt Whizz wrote labels
for them:

Coffee cake
with walnuts

Orange cake
with black
icing spiders

Banana and
honey cake
with
blackberries

Lemon cake
with strawberri
and cream

Chocolate
cake with
green icing
caterpillars

Coconut cake
with
marshmallows

Aunt Bimm cried happy tears. "I'm so proud of you both," she said.

Sunday was the day of the Tabletop Tasty Treats Sale. George's aunts took most of the cakes in their bicycle trailers. George put the last cake into a big tin and put a little box next to it. Milo sat in the trailer holding the tin and they set off. They stopped to look at the new copy of *MegaBuzz*. This week's cover looked especially interesting:

MegaBuzz

Terrifying but True - Snakes the Size of Dinosaurs!

Latest Photos from Deepest Space

Six Football Stickers to Collect

New Skateboard Moves - Impress Your Friends!

Free Magnifying Glass

But Nathan saw them. George whispered to Milo, "I thought he would turn up. Give me the cake tin and don't say anything. I've got a plan."

Nathan marched up to them. "Have you got a cake in that tin?" he demanded.

"Yes," said George, "but it isn't finished yet."

"Let me see it *now*!" Nathan yelled.

George opened the tin and Nathan's eyes nearly popped out with greed. George held up the little box. "I still have to add these decorations," he said.

"Hurry up then," Nathan snapped. "Do it *now* and give me that cake."

George sprinkled a few of the little red decorations on to the cake.

"I want *loads* of decorations," Nathan demanded. He grabbed the little box and emptied it on to the cake.

"Wait!" George shouted. "You don't want to do that!" But Nathan pulled the cake tin off him and started scoffing.

Milo gasped. "Oh no!" he thought. "I recognize those little red things. Those aren't cake decorations, they're super-red-hot chilli pepper flakes!"

Before George and Milo could stop
him, Nathan took three big bites:
CHOMP, CHOMP, CHOMP! Then
he took three more big bites: CHOMP,
CHOMP, CHOMP! Then he stopped.

George and Milo watched Nathan
change colour. He went pink, then red,
then purple, then he stuck out his tongue
and shouted, "AAAGH! AAAGH!
AAAGH!" Steam came out of his ears
and nose, and he jumped from one
foot to the other, shouting "AAAGH!
AAAGH! AAAGH!"

"Quick, Milo," said George. "Let's get
out of here!"

Chapter 10
Every Last Crumb

The Tabletop Tasty Treats Sale was so busy that George and Milo didn't have time to worry about Nathan. There was every kind of treat for sale – jam, biscuits, fudge, fruit pies, scones and, best of all, lots and lots of cakes. Everything sold very fast. Soon there was not a crumb left.

Nathan arrived with his dad but he didn't look at George or Milo.

"I think he might leave us alone now," said George.

"Yes, and we didn't *really* hurt him," said Milo. "He'll soon be eating cake again."

Nathan had had enough cake for one day but his dad was scoffing a great big slice.

At the end of the afternoon Aunt Mash added up the money George and Milo had made.

"You have enough for the next ten copies of *MegaBuzz*," she told them.

"Fantastic!" cried George and Milo.

"Can we keep baking cakes?" asked George. "Just to eat at home."

"Of course you can," said Aunt Bimm.

"How delicious!" said Aunt Whizz.

"And when you need more pocket money you can tidy my shed again, if you'd like to," said Aunt Mash. "Milo can help, too."

"Oh, yes please," said Milo.

"That would be brilliant," said George. "Thank you."

"Let's clear the table quickly," said Milo. "Then we can go and buy *MegaBuzz*."

At playtime on Monday, George and Milo read *MegaBuzz*. Nathan was standing on his own. He didn't look big and frightening any more. He just looked like a sad boy with no friends.

George nudged Milo. "Let's go and see if Nathan wants to play," he said quietly.

"I suppose we should," said Milo. "He does look unhappy."

George said sorry to Nathan for the super-red-hot chilli pepper trick and offered to shake hands, but Nathan walked away.

"Oh well. At least we tried to make friends," said George.

But at lunchtime Nathan came to find them. "I'd like to shake hands now, if you still want to," he said.

George, Milo and Nathan shook hands.

"Sorry I was such a bully," said Nathan. "And I'm glad you got *MegaBuzz!*"

He was going to walk away, but he stopped and looked shy. "Er ... I was wondering something," he said. "Would you show me how to bake a cake?"

George and Milo were very surprised. They looked at each other and nodded.

"Definitely," said George, smiling.

So, on Saturday they *all* got baking.

About the author

My first job was delivering newspapers on my bicycle. I got up very early every morning of the summer holidays and pedalled for miles with a big, heavy bag. I loved it!

I have done lots of other jobs since then and it was many years before I knew for certain that writing was what I loved best. Once you find what you really want to do there can be problems along the way, and even bullies who upset you, but if you keep going, and keep trying, not being put off by anything that comes along, you will always win in the end. You'll be happier and stronger, too.